GLENN ZOTTOLA
Bossa, Bonfá and Black Orpheus
...a tribute to Stan Getz

PLAYBACK+
Speed • Pitch • Balance • Loop

To access audio visit:
www.halleonard.com/mylibrary

Enter Code
1748-7711-7746-7748

ISBN 978-0-9890705-4-8

Music Minus One

EXCLUSIVELY DISTRIBUTED BY
HAL•LEONARD®

Visit Hal Leonard Online at
www.halleonard.com

Contact us:
Hal Leonard
7777 West Bluemound Road
Milwaukee, WI 53213
Email: info@halleonard.com

In Europe, contact:
Hal Leonard Europe Limited
42 Wigmore Street
Marylebone, London, W1U 2RN
Email: info@halleonardeurope.com

In Australia, contact:
Hal Leonard Australia Pty. Ltd.
4 Lentara Court
Cheltenham, Victoria, 3192 Australia
Email: info@halleonard.com.au

GLENN ZOTTOLA
Bossa, Bonfá and Black Orpheus
...a tribute to Stan Getz

CONTENTS

SOLO B♭ TENOR SAX

Black Orpheus

Luis Bonfá
and Antonio Carlos Jobim

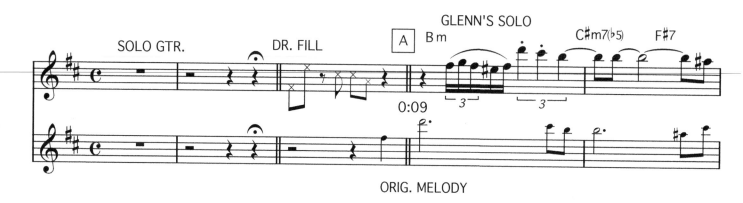

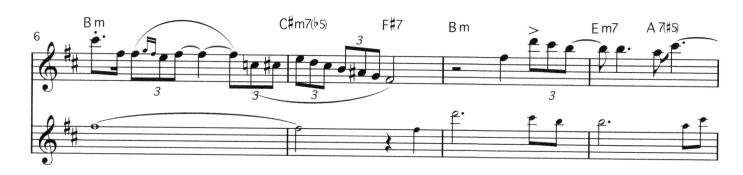

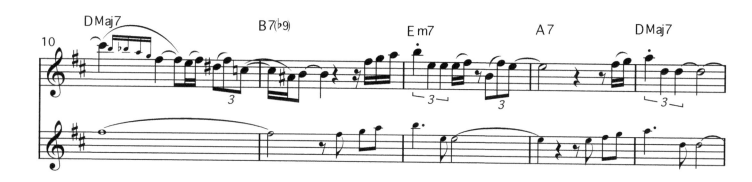

MMO 12225

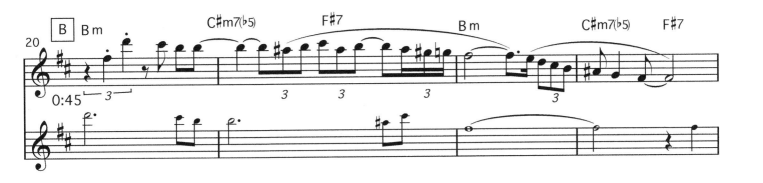

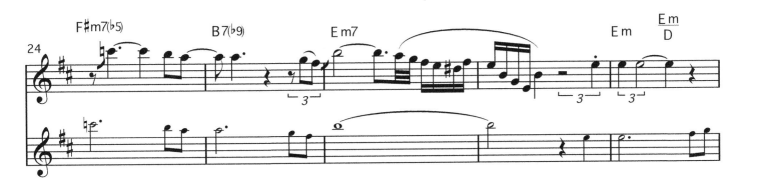

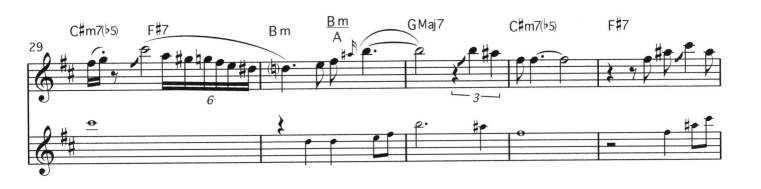

6

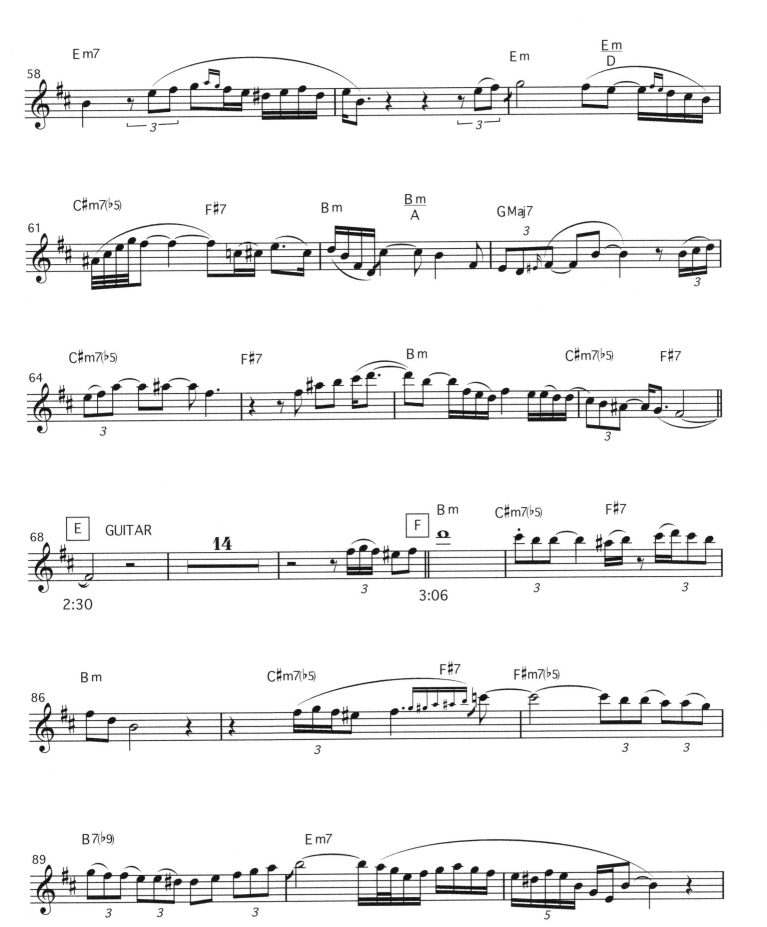

8

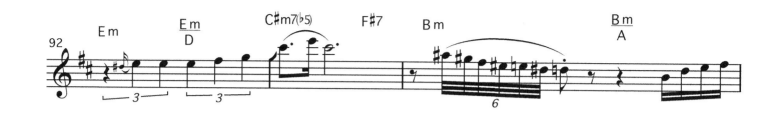

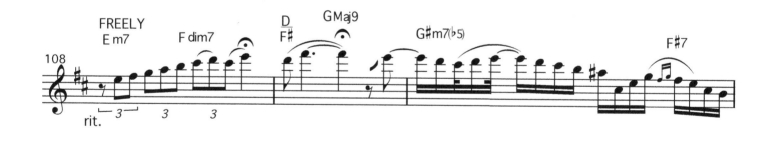

SOLO B♭ TENOR SAX

Girl From Ipanema

Music by Antonio Carlos Jobim
Words by Vinicius De Moraes and Norman Gimbel

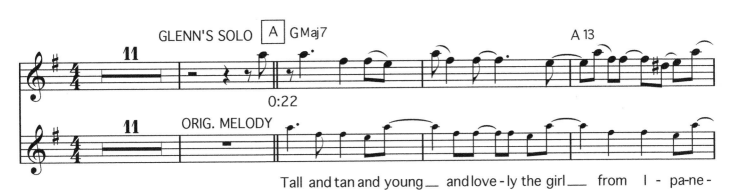

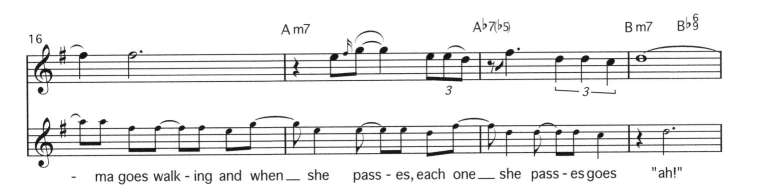

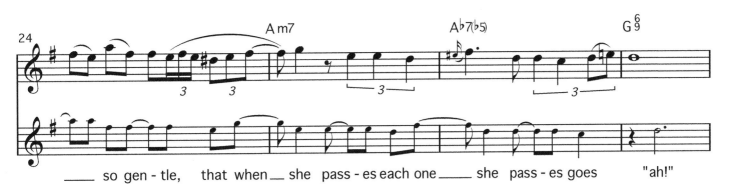

MMO 12225

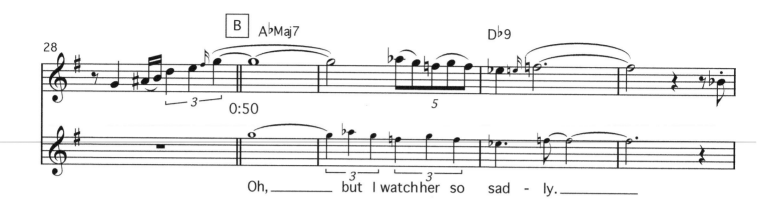

Oh, ____ but I watch her so sad - ly. ____

How ____ can I tell her I love her? ____ Yes ___

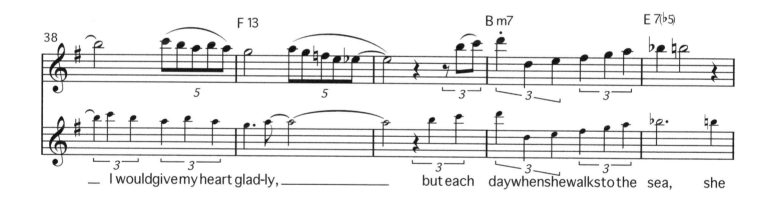

_ I would give my heart glad-ly, ____ but each day when she walks to the sea, she

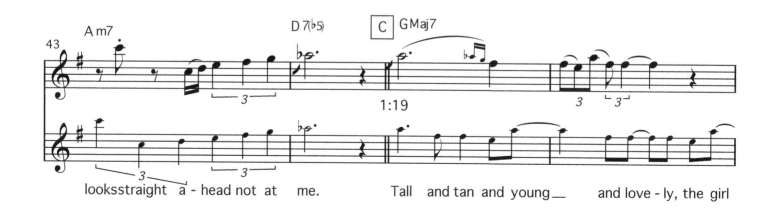

looks straight a - head not at me. Tall and tan and young __ and love - ly, the girl

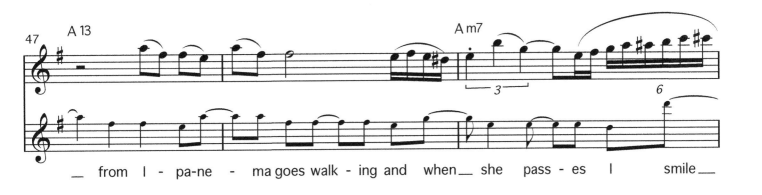

_ from I - pa-ne - ma goes walk - ing and when_ she pass - es I smile_

_ but she does - n't see.

SOLO B♭ TENOR SAX

Gentle Rain

Music by Luis Bonfá
Words by Matt Dubey

MMO 12225

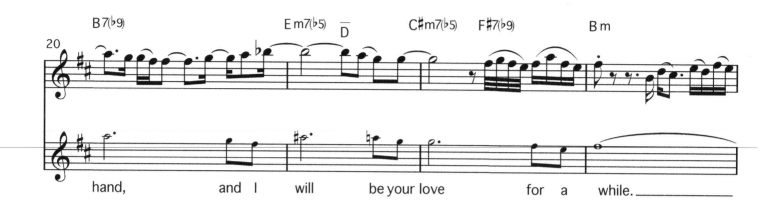

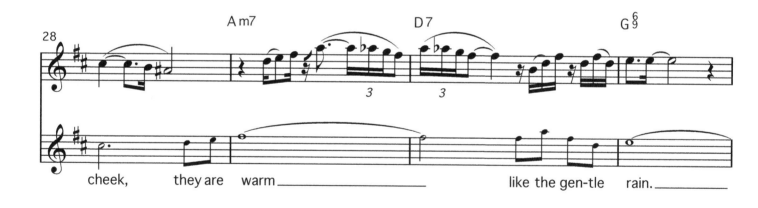

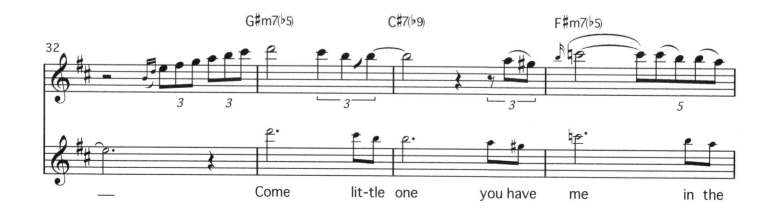

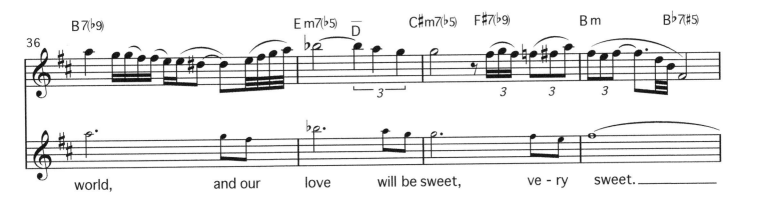

world, and our love will be sweet, ve - ry sweet._____

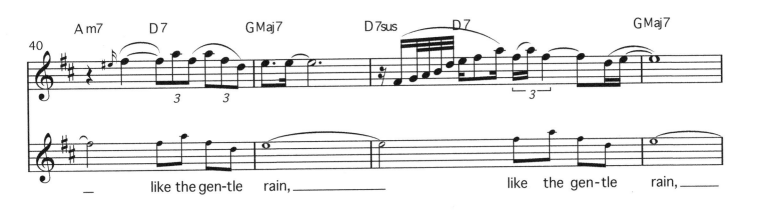

_ like the gen-tle rain,_____ like the gen-tle rain,_____

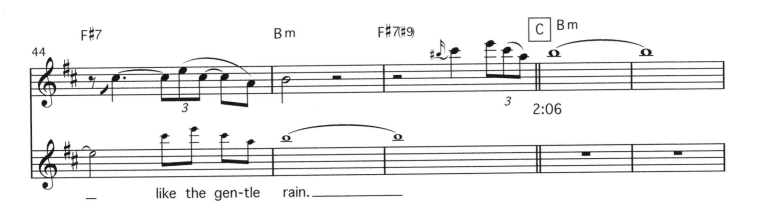

_ like the gen-tle rain._____

2:06

2:54

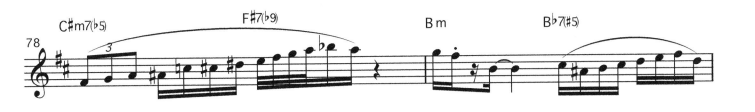

SOLO B♭ TENOR SAX

One Note Samba

Music by Antonio Carlos Jobim
Words by N. Mendonca

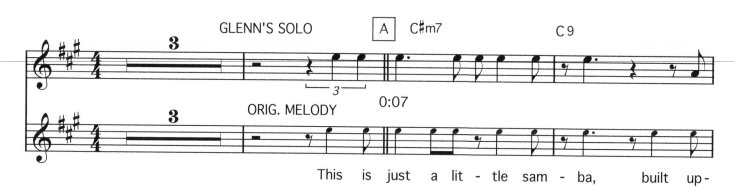

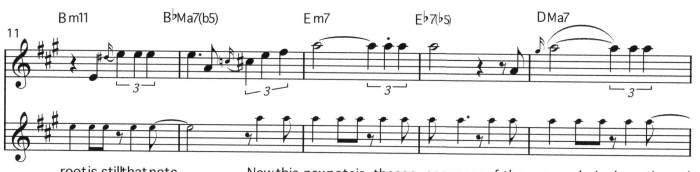

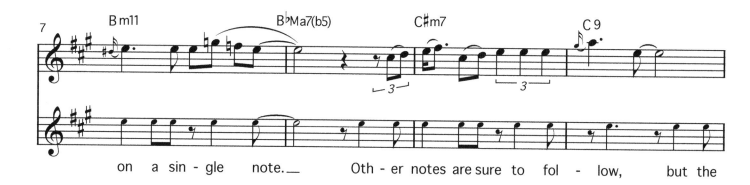

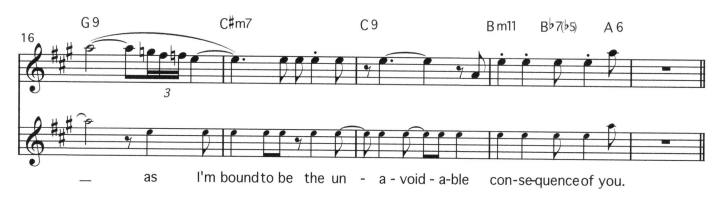

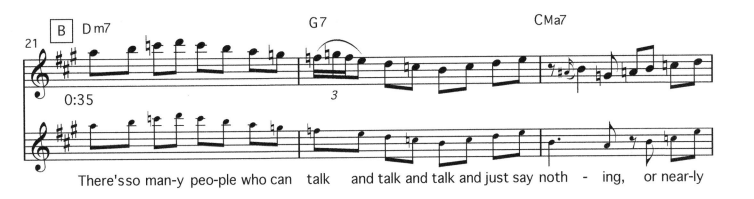

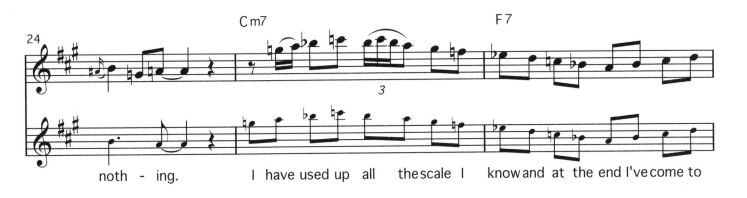

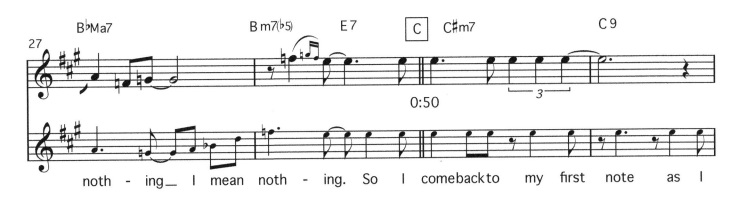

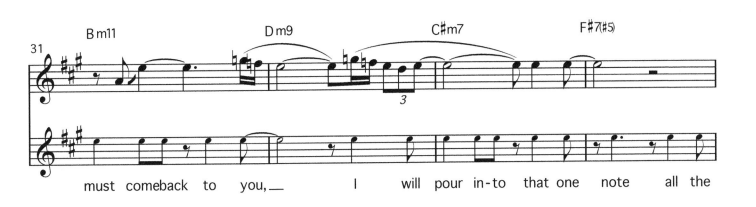

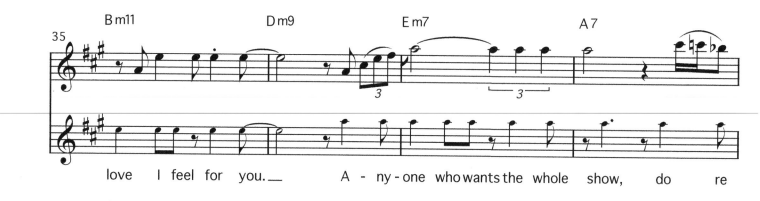

love I feel for you.___ A - ny - one who wants the whole show, do re

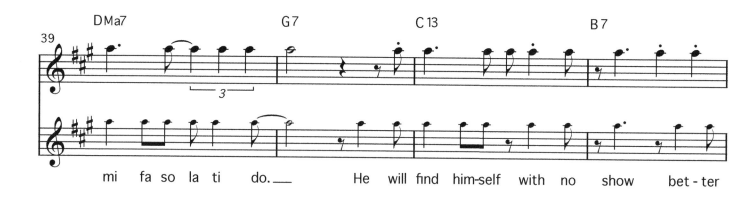

mi fa so la ti do.___ He will find him-self with no show bet - ter

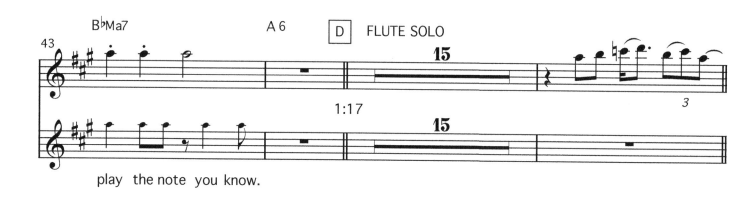

play the note you know.

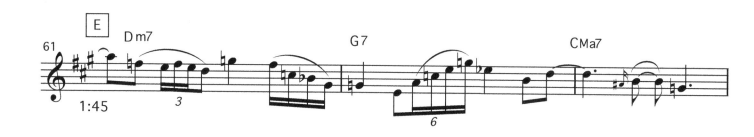

SOLO B♭ TENOR SAX

Once I Loved

Music by Antonio Carlos Jobim
English Words by Ray Gilbert
Original Words by Vinicius DeMoraes

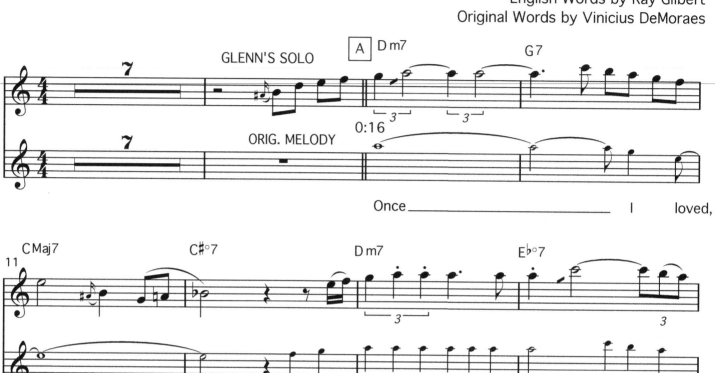

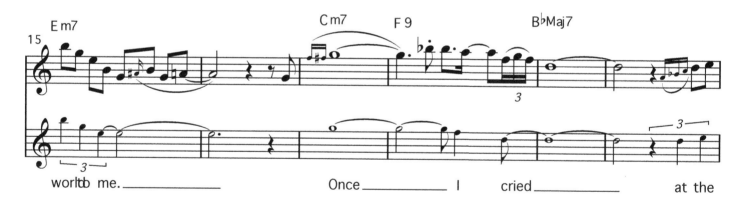

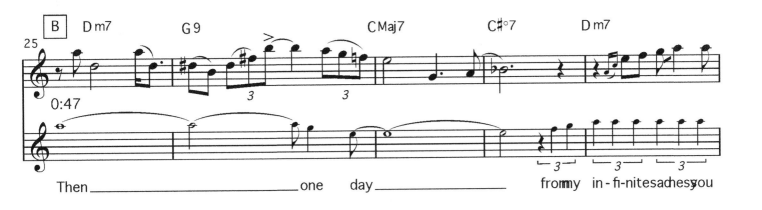

24

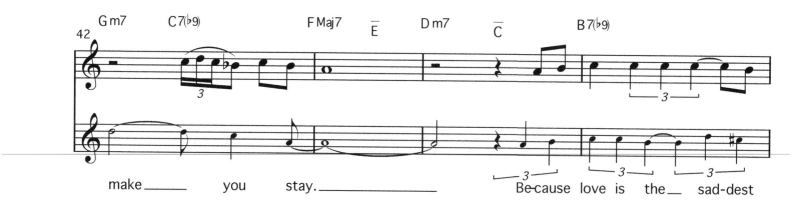

make_____ you stay._____ Be-cause love is the__ sad-dest

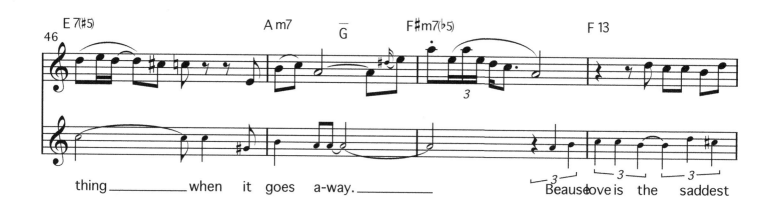

thing_____when it goes a-way._____ Beause love is the saddest

thing_____when it goes a - way._____

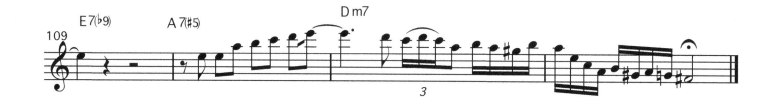

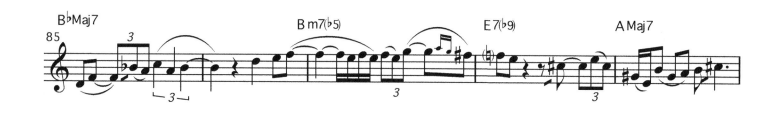

SOLO B♭ TENOR SAX

Dindi

Words and Music by Antonio Carlos Jobim,
Ray Gilbert and Oliveira Louis

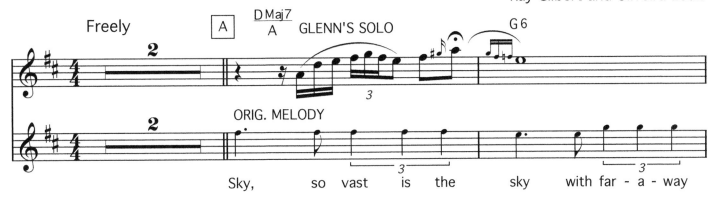

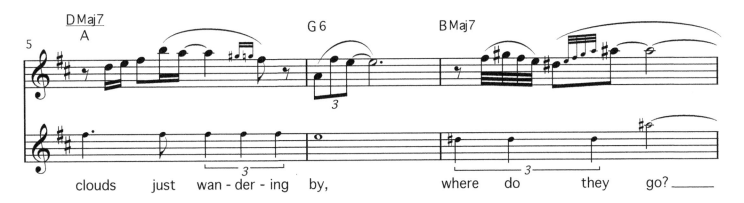

Sky, so vast is the sky with far - a - way clouds just wan - der - ing by, where do they go?

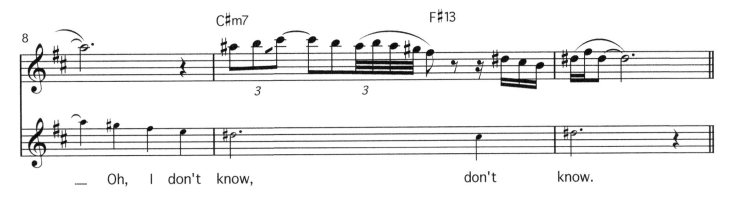

— Oh, I don't know, don't know.

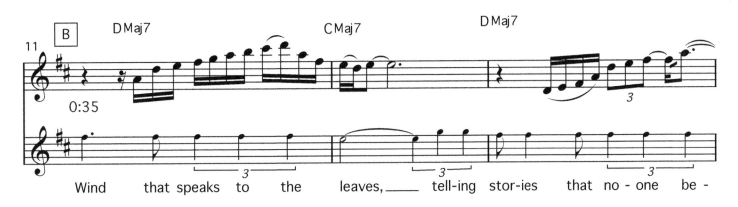

Wind that speaks to the leaves, tell-ing stor-ies that no - one be -

MMO 12225

lieves. Sto - ries of love _____ be - long to

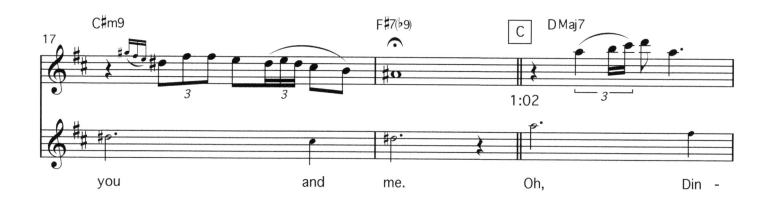

you and me. Oh, Din -

di, if I on - ly had words I would say all the beau - ti - ful

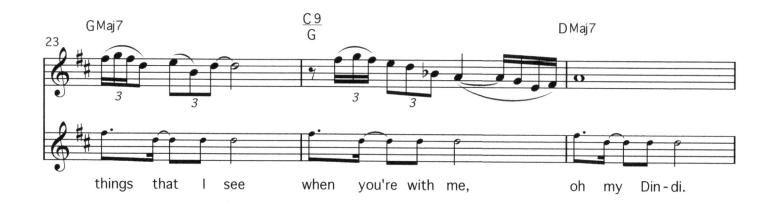

things that I see when you're with me, oh my Din - di.

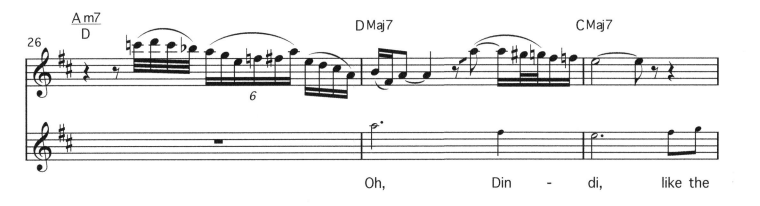

Oh, Din - di, like the

song of the wind in the trees, that's how my heart is sing-ing, Din-di,

hap - py Din - di, when you're with me.

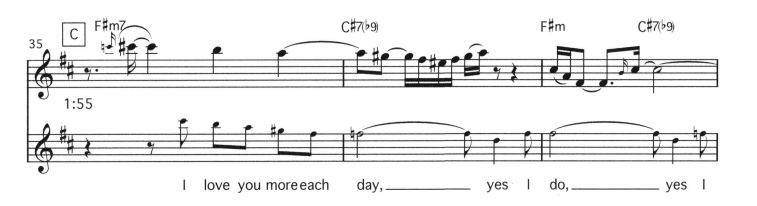

I love you more each day,_____ yes I do,_____ yes I

do.   I'd let you go a - way_____ if you

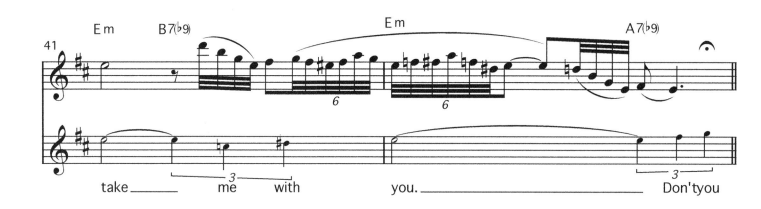

take_____ me with you._____ Don't you

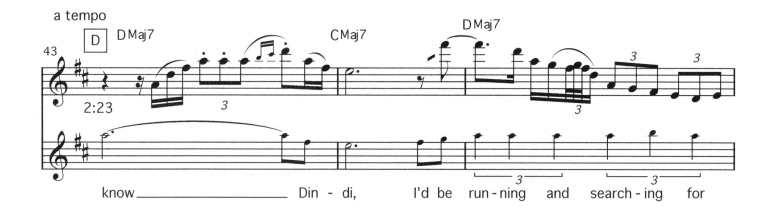

know_____ Din - di, I'd be run - ning and search - ing for

you like a riv-er that can't find the sea,   that would be me with-out

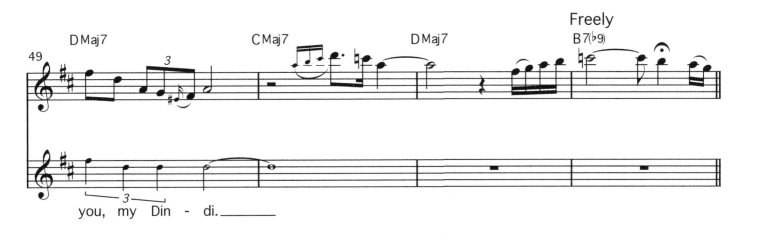

you, my Din - di. _____

2:55

SOLO B♭ TENOR SAX

Baubles, Bangles and Beads

Robert Wright and George Forrest

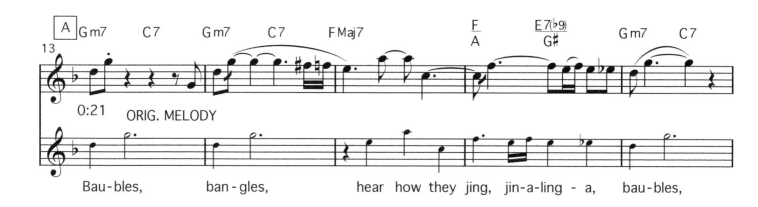

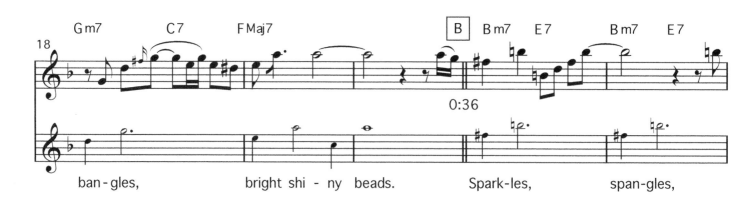

34

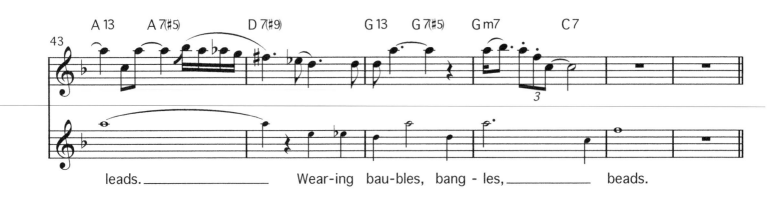

leads. _____ Wear-ing bau-bles, bang - les, _____ beads.

1:27

2:12

(FADE)

SOLO B♭ TENOR SAX

Meditation

Antonio Carlos Jobim

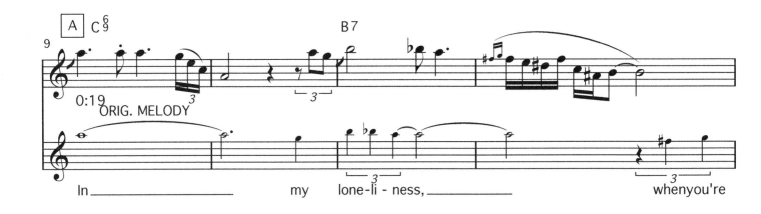

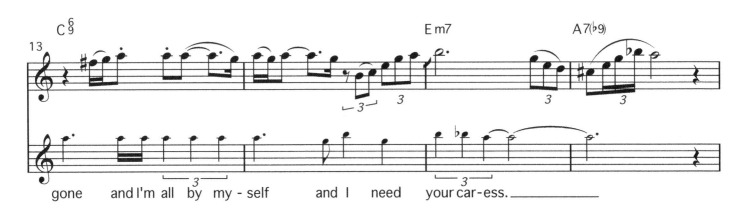

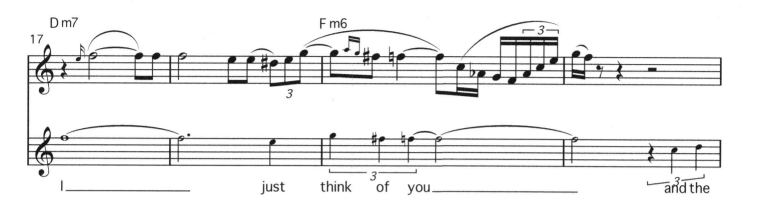

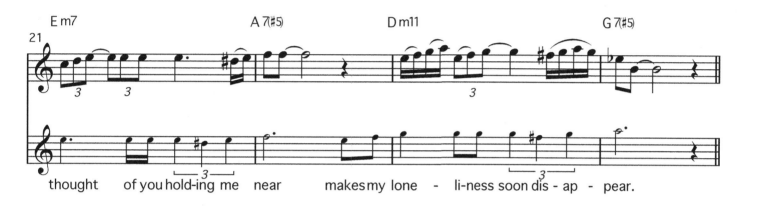

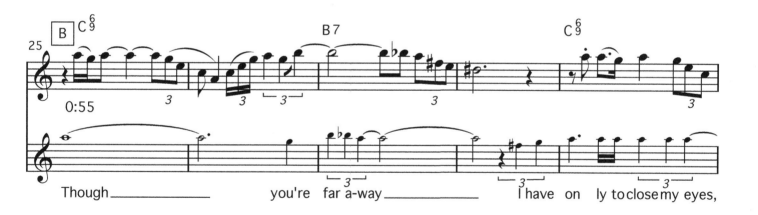

just close my eyes, _____ and the

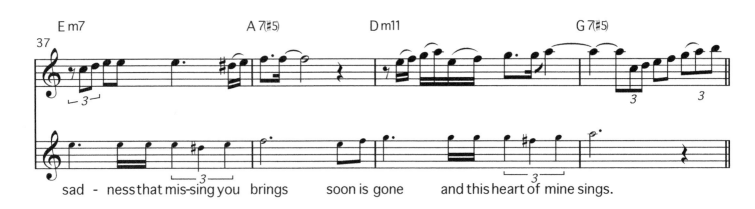

sad - ness that mis-sing you brings soon is gone and this heart of mine sings.

Yes, _____ I love you so, _____ and that for me _ is

all I need to know. _____

SOLO B♭ TENOR SAX

Triste

Antonio Carlos Jobim

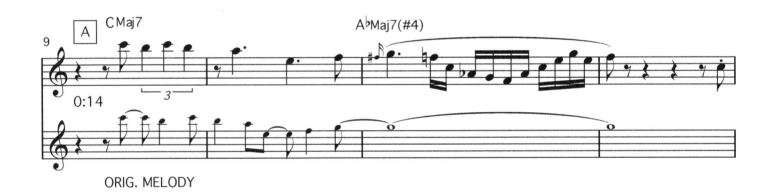

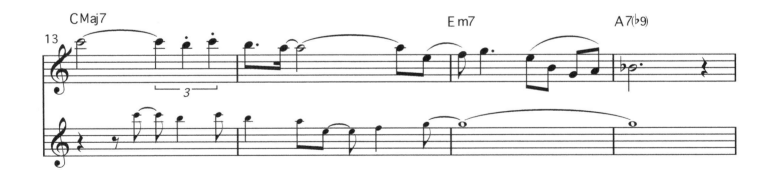

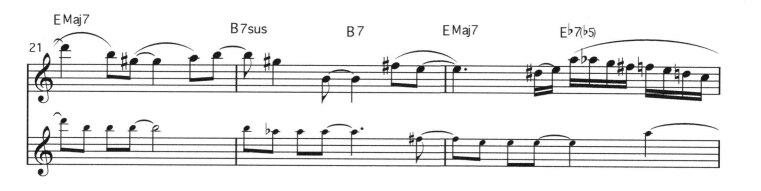

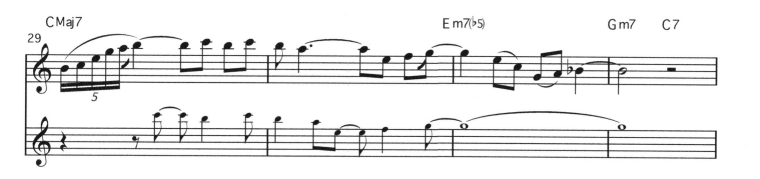

1:12

1:37

SOLO B♭ TENOR SAX

I Concentrate On You

Cole Porter

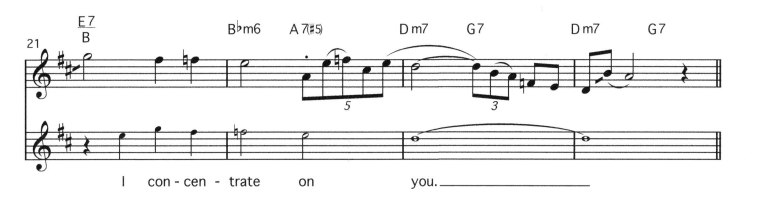

I con - cen - trate on you._____

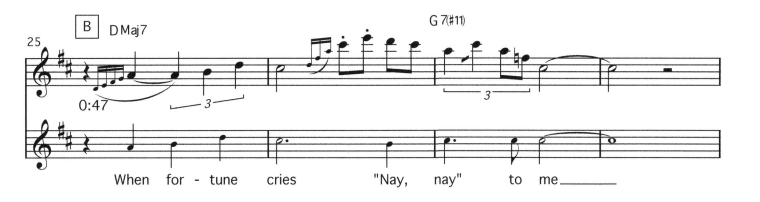

When for - tune cries "Nay, nay" to me_____

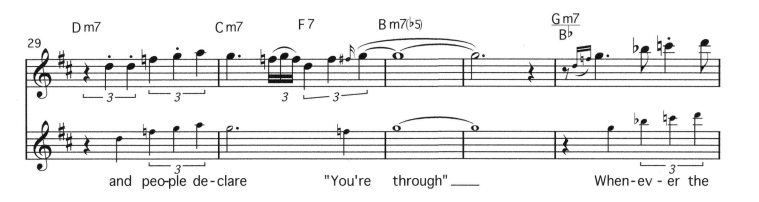

and peo-ple de-clare "You're through" _____ When-ev - er the

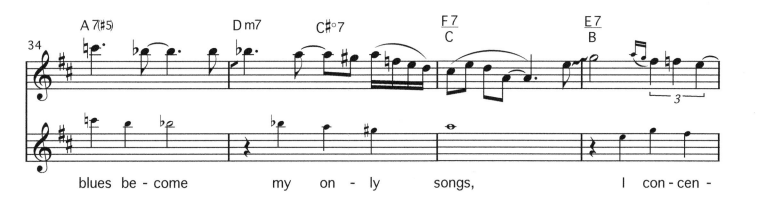

blues be - come my on - ly songs, I con - cen -

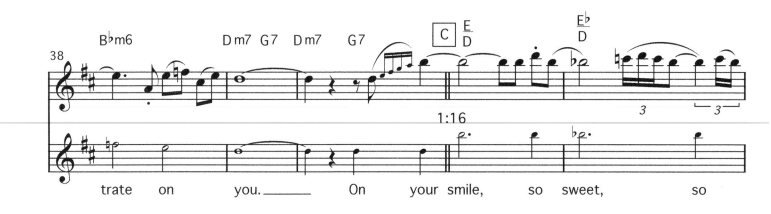

trate on you._____ On your smile, so sweet, so

ten - der_____ when at first my kiss you de - cline._____

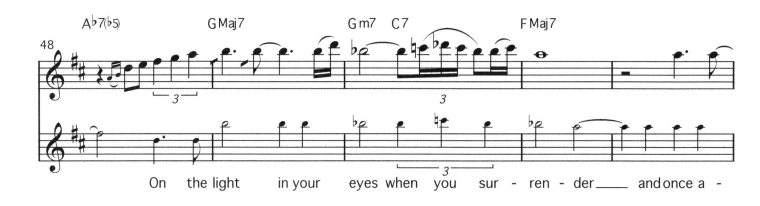

On the light in your eyes when you sur - ren - der_____ and once a -

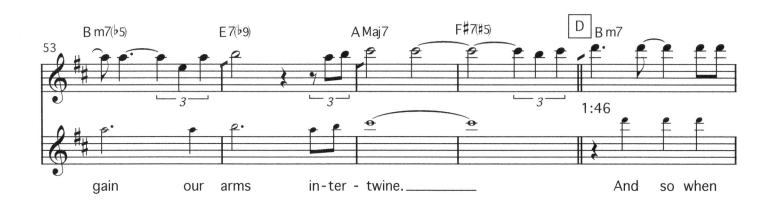

gain our arms in - ter - twine._____ And so when

SOLO B♭ TENOR SAX

Samba De Orfeu

Music by Luis Bonfá
Words by Antonio Maria

GLENN ZOTTOLA

"This album was truly a joy to do. The idea for the album was reinforced by a conversation I had with John Travolta at a party several years ago. I was talking to John about Stan Getz and how I wanted to do a bossa album. Suddenly he broke out into song, singing a Jobim bossa beautifully. I was surprised and asked him about this. He said that he was a big fan of Stan Getz and his music, saying 'I am a child of the 60s.' Now years later, I felt it was an appropriate time to revisit this timeless, gentle and classic music that broke onto the music scene during a very turbulent time. These songs provide me a 'canvas' similar to the great standards of the American songbook. They should be a part of every player's and singer's repertoire regardless of the style they wish to pursue. I was very fortunate to receive an exact copy of Stan Getz's actual tenor saxophone mouthpiece from RS Berkeley for this project. I used it on this album to create the 'timbre' on my horn that caught everyone's ear at that time. I would like to thank my brother Bob, who is a great admirer of Stan's playing and the bossa nova, for all his help in producing this album, and as always Irv Kratka, for his tireless support in forwarding the great American songbook."

- Glenn Zottola

If you would like to communicate with Glenn Zottola, go to
www.glennzottola.com

Glenn Zottola's tribute to bossa nova, Antonio Carlos Jobim and Stan Getz brings back the timeless beauty of Brazilian jazz from the late 1950s and 1960s.

Antonio Carlos Jobim (1927-94) can be considered the last of the major composers of the Great American Songbook even though he was not from the United States. During 1915-60, hundreds of standards were composed by the likes of Irving Berlin, Jerome Kern, George Gershwin, Cole Porter, Harold Arlen, Richard Rodgers, Duke Ellington, Fats Waller, Hoagy Carmichael, Harry Warren and a dozen other brilliant songwriters. The rise of rock and roll and singer/songwriters (who primarily performed their own material) along with the decline of radio, big bands and eventually Broadway ended this golden era. Jobim with the many classic bossa novas that he wrote helped extend the period of the Great American Songbook throughout the 1960s, adding many fresh and highly appealing standards to the repertoire of both singers and instrumentalists in the jazz and pop worlds.

Jobim was born in Rio de Janiero as part of a prominent family that included a father who was a diplomat, journalist and professor. After his parents separated when he was young, he grew up with his mother in the beachside neighborhood Ipanema and was given his first piano by his stepfather. Jobim was originally trained to become an architect but he changed his mind. By the time he was 20, he was working in nightclubs as a pianist.

After a few years of freelancing as a pianist, in 1954 he made his first record, accompanying singer Bill Farr. By then Jobim was leading *"Tom and his Band"* (Tom was his nickname), working as an arranger for a recording label, and gradually becoming popular locally. During this time, Jobim also began to write songs. His music was influenced by a variety of different sources. The pioneering Brazilian composers Pixinguinha and Heitor Villa-Lobos and the French classical composers Claude Debussy and Maurice Ravel made a strong impression on Jobim. So too did the West Coast cool jazz of Gerry Mulligan, Chet Baker and Stan Getz, along with the samba rhythms of Brazilian popular music.

In 1956, Jobim and lyricist Vinicius de Moraes collaborated to write a large part of the score for a play, *Orfeo do Carnaval*. Two years later when the production was being turned into the film *Black Orpheus*, producer Sacha Gordine decided against using any of the music from the play. Instead he wanted Jobim and Moraes to write a new score but, because Moraes was working for the Brazilian Ministry of Foreign Affairs in Uruguay and was mostly unavailable, the team of Jobim and Moraes only wrote three songs, best known of which was *"A Felicidade."* Instead, Luiz Bonfá composed most of the music for the film.

Bonfá (1922-2001), who was also from Rio de Janeiro, was a brilliant guitarist who had been prominent in Brazil since 1947 when he was featured on the radio. Some of his songs were recorded in the 1950s by Brazilian singer Dick Farney, which resulted in Bonfá becoming acquainted with Jobim. While he contributed a few numbers to the play *Orfeu da Carnival*, he ended up writing the bulk of the songs for the *Black Orpheus* film. The movie's two most memorable tunes, *"Manha de Carnival (A Day In The Life Of A Fool)"* and *"Samba de Orfeu"* are both Bonfá's and rank as the first bossa nova tunes to become standards. While most of Bonfá's other compositions from later years (other than *"Gentle Rain"*) never gained the popularity and exposure of those two songs, he had a long career as a notable guitarist. Bonfá performed at the famous bossa nova Carnegie Hall concert in Nov. 1962 (an event that introduced many of the top Brazilian performers to American audiences) and stayed active both in Brazil and the United States as a performer until shortly before his death.

The release of *Black Orpheus*, which won the 1960 Academy Award for Best Foreign Language Film, was one the first times that Brazilian jazz was heard in the United States. The film, based on the Greek legend of Orpheus and Eurydice, was partly shot during Carnaval in Rio de Janeiro. Both the music and the infectious dancing were among the most memorable ingredients of the production.

While Black Orpheus was a good introduction to the new Brazilian style, the music would have remained a regional style if it had not had a charismatic performer to help introduce the songs. While Jobim was a decent pianist, guitarist and singer, he was not as comfortable with live performing and touring as he was with composing and recording. It would fall to Joao Gilberto to bring out the beauty in Jobim's songs.

Gilberto, who was born in 1931 and is still active today, began playing guitar when he was 14. He worked as a singer on the radio as a teenager and in 1950 moved to Rio de Janeiro where at first he worked with the vocal group Garotos da Lua. While he made his recording debut in 1951, he struggled for several years in obscurity and poverty. During this period, Gilberto developed a very personal vocal and guitar style that was both introverted and haunting, using gentle rhythms that were similar to what Jobim was developing. He wrote "Bim Bom" which was possibly the earliest bossa nova song. In 1956 he met Jobim and they were both very impressed with each other's complementary musical style. Two years later Gilberto, with his whispery singing, introduced Jobim's "Chega de Saudade (No More Blues)" on a recording that was included in the 1959 Lp of the same name. The album sold extremely well, helping lead to the popularity of bossa nova in Brazil. Other Gilberto records followed.

It would still be a little time before bossa nova reached the United States. Visiting Americans who heard the music in Brazil were enthusiastic about the new style, including flutist Herbie Mann and most notably guitarist Charlie Byrd (1925-99). Byrd was already considered an unusual guitarist in the jazz world because, although very familiar with Charlie Christian, he was more strongly influenced by both Django Reinhardt and the classical guitarist Andres Segovia (with whom he had studied). By the late 1950s, Byrd was playing and recording jazz in the Washington D.C. area, specializing in the acoustic guitar. His repertoire included classical pieces and traditional songs from Brazil. In the spring of 1961, Byrd toured South America (including Brazil) for the State Department and returned home very enthusiastic about the new bossa nova music. Back in the U.S., he introduced Stan Getz to the recordings of Jobim and Gilberto. Getz became very enthusiastic and the two agreed to collaborate on a recording project.

The resulting album, which was released in 1962, was *Jazz Samba*. To everyone's surprise it not only entered Billboard's pop charts but by March 1963 was the #1 selling album. A single, "*Desafinado*," was a huge hit and it launched a bossa nova craze in the United States. Soon it seemed as if every performer, whether they understood the subtleties of Brazilian melodies and rhythms or not, was releasing a bossa nova album. While Byrd and Getz never worked together again, Charlie Byrd became one of the major interpreters of bossa nova, helping through his performances and recordings to make many of the Jobim songs into standards.

Stan Getz (1927-91) had already had a remarkable career before he became involved in bossa nova. He was a professional with major bands by 1943 when as a 16-year old he was with the Jack Teagarden Orchestra. Getz worked with Stan Kenton, Jimmy Dorsey and Benny Goodman before gaining fame as one of the "*Four Brothers*" with Woody Herman's Second Herd during 1947-49. His solo on "*Early Autumn*" helped to introduce his beautiful Lester Young-inspired tone. In the 1950s Getz was heard in many settings including a classic quintet with guitarist Jimmy Raney, a hit recording of "*Moonlight In Vermont*" with guitarist Johnny Smith, recordings with Dizzy Gillespie, appearances with Jazz At The Philharmonic, and a period spent in Europe.

Getz had the perfect tone on his tenor for bossa nova, gentle and light while he caressed the warm melodies. His tenor seemed to emulate the singing style of Joao Gilberto. After recording *Jazz Samba*, Getz explored bossa nova for the next two years. He recorded *Big Band Bossa Nova* (with arrangements by Gary McFarland), *Jazz Samba Encore* with Luiz Bonfá, and co-led Stan Getz/Laurindo Almeida with the great Brazilian guitarist Almeida.

In 1963, when the market was very saturated with bossa nova recordings, Stan Getz went back to the original source, teaming up with Antonio Carlos Jobim (heard on piano) and singer-guitarist Joao Gilberto for Getz/Gilberto. The most famous song on both this album and in bossa nova history came together a bit by accident. "The Girl From Ipanema" features Gilberto's singing in Portuguese and Getz's tenor. However it was felt that it should also have a vocal in English. Since Joao Gilberto did not know English very well, his wife Astrud Gilberto (born in 1940), who had never sung professionally before, was pressed into service at the last minute. Her simple and basic delivery, which was quietly sensuous, was the secret weapon that made "The Girl From Ipanema" into a million seller. Also featured on this album were such numbers as "*Corcovado (Quiet Nights of Quiet Stars)*", "*So Danco Samba*" and a vocal version of "*Desafinado*."

Bossa nova had hit its height. Joao Gilberto and Astrud Gilberto (even aft they were divorced) had major international careers and Antonio Carl Jobim permanently became a household name. Within a few years of Get Gilberto, the rise of the Beatles and rock had completely overshadowed bos nova and it was no longer on the pop charts. However the music is no considered a classic style and its best songs are standards that are still belov and performed today.

Glenn Zottola is best known as a hot swing jazz trumpeter who has occ sionally played alto, but on this project he performs melodic versions of 1 bossa nova classics on tenor. "Although I always loved the tenor, whether was Sonny Rollins or Lester Young, I only really started digging into the teno few years ago. For this project, I used a duplicate of Stan Getz's mouthpiece. N goal was to get as close to his beautiful sound as possible. I love how Stan, w had monster chops, scaled himself back during his bossa nova performanc to adopt a really appropriate and melodic approach, keeping it simple a beautiful. Stan Getz saw what bossa nova was about and he fit his sound in the understated and gentle music."

The program begins with Luiz Bonfá's "*Manha de Carnival (A Day In The L Of A Fool)*" from *Black Orpheus*, the song that for many Americans in the la 1950s/early '60s was the first time that they heard a bossa nova. As is true e each of these performances, Glenn Zottola's sound, while purposely close to th of Stan Getz's, also includes a bit of his own musical personality. He utiliz Getz's melodic approach, caressing the theme while improvising in subtle wa through his phrasing, use of space and timing.

"*The Girl From Ipanema*," bossa nova's most popular song, is played bea tifully by Zottola. Not known to many listeners is that the main part of t melody utilizes the same chord changes as "*Take The 'A' Train*" although t middle section (the bridge) is quite original. More than a half century since i introduction, the melody of "*The Girl From Ipanema*" is still one of the mo famous in the world.

"*Gentle Rain*," written by Luiz Bonfá for the 1965 film *The Gentle Rain*, h been recorded by many singers through the years including Barbra Streisa and Irene Kral. Zottola puts a great deal of quiet emotion into this version.

Although "*One Note Samba*" has had many vocal versions through t years, including Joao Gilberto in 1960, the most famous rendition was t instrumental performance by Getz and Charlie Byrd on *Jazz Samba*. Zotto wisely sticks closely to the melody.

"*Once I Loved*" (or "*O Amor Em Paz*") was introduced by Joao Gilberto 1961 and performed by Jobim himself on piano on a 1963 recording. Zottola conversational playing sounds a bit as if he is speaking to the listener.

"*Dindi*" was written by Jobim in 1966 for the Brazilian singer Sylvia Tell whose nickname was Dindi. The thoughtful melody was recorded through t years by everyone from Sinatra to Wayne Shorter, Sarah Vaughan to Willie Bob

"*Baubles, Bangles And Beads*," a swing standard from 1953, was transform into bossa nova on the classic album *Frank Sinatra & Antonio Carlos Jobim*. is an example of how most swing tunes could become a bossa nova if given t right type of rhythms. It also points out Jobim's ties to the jazz tradition.

Jobim's "*Meditation (Meditacao)*" is one of those songs whose melody more familiar than its title. It is one of the more beautiful bossa nova tune One of its earlier versions was by Cal Tjader in 1962.

"*Triste*," which means "sad" in Portuguese, was recorded by Jobim in 1967. with many bossa novas, the melody is both quietly joyful and a bit melanchol

Also from the *Frank Sinatra & Antonio Carlos Jobim* album, "*I Concentrate C You*" is given a bossa nova treatment that could lead one into believing that was written in Brazil in 1960 rather than by Cole Porter in 1940 New Yor

Concluding this highly enjoyable set of classic bossa novas is Luiz Bonfá "*Samba De Orfeu*," given an infectious version by Glenn Zottola that brin us back to the beginnings of bossa nova.

More than 50 years after "*The Girl From Ipanema*," bossa nova is a permane part of American music, and Antonio Carlos Jobim is recognized as one of t greatest songwriters of the 20th century. Glenn Zottola does the music justic

Scott Yanow, *author of 11 books includi The Great Jazz Guitarists, The Jazz Singe Jazz On Film and Jazz On Record 1917-7*